LOONS

John Woodward

Grolier
an imprint of

SCHOLASTIC

www.scholastic.com/librarypublishing

Published 2008 by Grolier
An imprint of Scholastic Library Publishing
Old Sherman Turnpike, Danbury,
Connecticut 06816

For The Brown Reference Group plc
Project Editor: Jolyon Goddard
Copy-editors: Lesley Ellis, Lisa Hughes,
    Wendy Horobin
Picture Researcher: Clare Newman
Designers: Jeni Child, Lynne Ross,
    Sarah Williams
Managing Editor: Bridget Giles

Volume ISBN-13: 978-0-7172-6258-8
Volume ISBN-10: 0-7172-6258-8

**Library of Congress
Cataloging-in-Publication Data**

Nature's children. Set 2.
    p. cm.
  Includes bibliographical references and
index.
  ISBN-13: 978-0-7172-8081-0
  ISBN-10: 0-7172-8081-0
  1. Animals--Encyclopedias, Juvenile. 1.
Grolier (Firm)
  QL49.N383 2007
  590--dc22
                        2007026928

Printed and bound in China

PICTURE CREDITS

Front Cover: **Nature PL**: Paul Hobson

Back Cover: **Nature PL**: John Cancalosi;
NHPA: Tom Kitchin and Vicki Hurst, Fari
Peltomaki

Alamy: Rick and Nora Bowers 13, Steven J.
Kazlowski 14, 42, 46, Chris Sutton 18, David
Tipling 4, 33, 45; **FLPA**: Mike Jones 34,
Michael Quinton/Minden Pictures 38, 41,
Albert Visage 29; **Nature PL**: Paul Hobson
21; **Photos.com**: 6; **Shutterstock**: Bull's-
Eye Arts 2–3, 26–27, 30, Sebastien Gauthier
5, Ronnie Howard 10, Brad Thompson 37;
Still Pictures: Tom Vezo 17, 22;
Superstock: Age Fotostock 9.

Contents

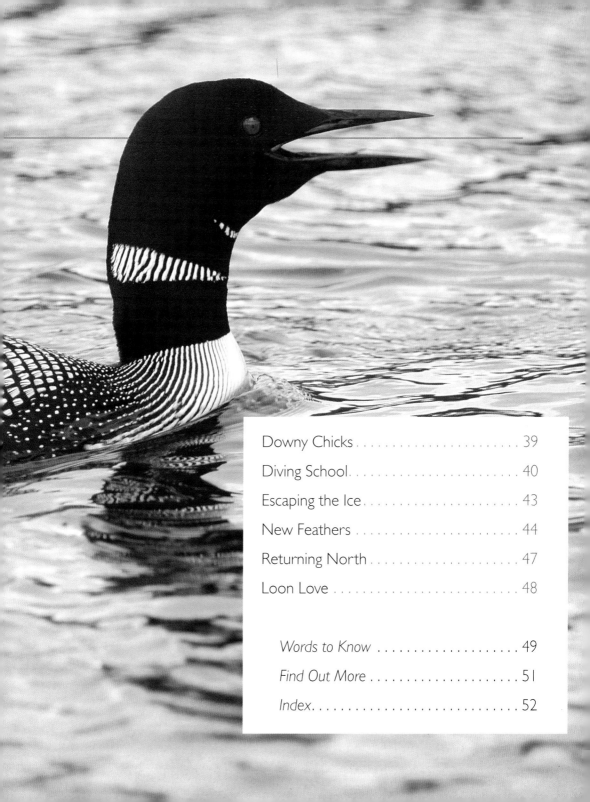

FACT FILE: Loons

Class	Birds (Aves)
Order	Loonlike birds (Gaviiformes)
Family	Loon family (Gaviidae)
Genus	*Gavia*
Species	Common loon (*Gavia immer*), red-throated loon (*Gavia stellata*), Arctic loon (*Gavia arctica*), Pacific loon (*Gavia pacifica*), and yellow-billed loon (*Gavia adamsii*)
World distribution	North America, Greenland, Iceland, Britain, Scandinavia, Russia, Siberia, and the Arctic
Habitat	Northern lakes in summer, where it breeds; southern lakes and coasts in winter
Distinctive physical characteristics	Loons have a long body, a heavy, sharp-pointed beak, legs at the back of their body, and webbed feet; in summer the common loon has a black head and neck, with a striped collar and a checkered black-and-white back; in winter it is grayer with a pale face
Habits	Lives alone or in pairs; dives underwater to feed; nests onshore; flies south for winter
Diet	Fish, frogs, crustaceans, insects, and weeds

Introduction

There are five different types, or species, of loons. The birds are all very similar, apart from their feather colors and patterns. Loons behave much like large ducks. But they are better equipped than ducks for chasing fish and other animals underwater. A loon's legs are perfect for swimming and diving, but they are almost useless on land. Loons find walking extremely difficult and as a result, they spend most of their time on water. Male common loons are famous for their haunting calls, especially in summer when the sounds echo over the northern lakes where they **breed**.

A common loon swims on a lake.

A loon chick
hitches a ride on
its parent's back.

Baby Loons

When loon chicks hatch they are fluffy and active, unlike some other baby birds. They can swim when they are only a few hours old. But the first chick to hatch does not go far until its brother or sister hatches, too. Then both chicks leave the nest and swim around on the lake, following their mother and father. The adult loons are careful not to swim too fast for the babies. They also watch out for any danger. If a chick gets cold or tired, it may ride on its parent's back. If the adult decides to dive underwater the chick hops off!

A Family Tree

The common loon has four close relatives in its family. Some of them can be difficult to tell apart. The yellow-billed loon of northern North America looks very similar to the common loon, except for its yellow beak, or bill. The Arctic loon and the Pacific loon look very similar to each other. Both have a gray head and beautiful black-and-white stripes on their neck in summer. The Arctic loon lives in northern Asia. In summer, the Pacific loon lives in Alaska and northern Canada. In winter, it lives on the Pacific coast.

The red-throated loon is the most unique-looking. It is the smallest and slimmest of the loons, and has a distinctive rusty-red throat in summer. It lives in the Arctic in summer and moves south along ocean shores for winter.

A red-throated loon, perched on a mud nest, looks after its chick.

The common loon
has bold feather
patterns during
the summer
breeding season.

Common Loon

The common loon is a very striking bird in summer, with a sleek black head, sharp black beak, and red eyes. At this time, the rest of its feathers form a distinctive black-and-white pattern, creating a checkerboard effect on the loon's back and a striped "necklace" around its throat.

Male and female common loons look the same. Their beautiful summer **plumage** makes them more attractive to each other. But their bold patterns also make them more obvious to **predators**. Luckily when the breeding season is over, their feathers become more muted and the birds are better able to blend in with their surroundings.

Winter Gray

In late summer, a common loon **molts** its boldly patterned feathers and grows new ones for the winter. This winter plumage is much grayer and not so boldly patterned. Instead of a black head, black beak, and a striped neck, the loon has a dark gray head, a grayish white face, and a paler beak. Its back still has a checkered pattern, but in two shades of gray feathers.

The loon's winter plumage makes it look completely different. Without its distinct markings it is difficult to identify a loon in the wild. Yet that is when most people are likely to see a loon. These birds stay in the far north during summer and visit southern shores near big cities only in winter.

A loon's winter plumage is less colorful compared with its summer one.

**A pair of loons meet
on a partly frozen lake.**

Lakes and Seashores

Common loons live in very different places depending on the time of year. In summer, they live on and around lakes in North America, particularly Canada, and from North Dakota to Maine. They can also be found in Greenland, Iceland, and some parts of Europe. These places are where they nest and raise their young. But when these northern lakes freeze over in late fall, the loons can no longer hunt for fish and other animals in the water. At this time of year, the loons fly away, or **migrate**, to places where the water is not frozen.

Most common loons move to coasts, where the salty ocean water does not freeze, except in the far north. Some North American common loons travel as far south as southern California, Texas, and Florida. Because they have lost their striking black-and-white summer coat by this time, the loons are not easily recognized. As a result, common loons are often mistaken for other birds.

Fine Feathers

A loon's feathers grow so close together that water cannot get through them. The tightly knit feathers also trap warm air between them, which stops the bird from becoming cold. The trapped air acts much like a life jacket, helping the loon to float on the water. And of course, the bird's feathers help it to fly, too. But the feathers cannot do these things if they are dirty or tangled. The loon has to look after its feathers by preening, or washing out any dirt, and waterproofing them with special oil.

The oil comes from a **preen gland** near the bird's tail. The loon takes some oil on its beak and carefully rubs it on each feather. At the same time, the bird tidies and straightens the feathers so they are able to do their job properly. It does that every day to keep itself clean and healthy.

This Pacific loon has
carefully preened
its feathers.

A common loon paddles with its feet while it looks for food.

Expert Divers

A loon's head and body are perfectly **streamlined**, and it can swim underwater easily. The loon pushes itself along with its large **webbed feet**. The feet are positioned right at the back of its body and work like the propeller of a submarine. The loon pushes with both feet at once, moving forward in a series of surges. A loon can swim as far as a city block in less than a minute. It can also dive right to the bottom of a lake.

Loons usually dive quickly and quietly, leaving just a few ripples behind. If you see a loon dive, try to figure out where it might come to the surface again. It's not easy!

The Loon on Land

The loon is a fast, graceful swimmer because its legs are set so far back on its body. But the position of its legs also makes the bird extremely clumsy on land because it cannot balance properly. It shuffles along awkwardly and slowly, and may even fall over onto its stomach. After only a short distance, the loon gets very tired. At this point the loon is an easy target for predators, such as lynx and mink.

Wisely, loons stay in the water most of the time. They come on land only when they are nesting. They build their nests as close as possible to the water. That way they can easily dive into the lake to escape any danger.

A red-throated loon stays alert as it sits with its chicks.

A common loon
sinks up to its
neck in the water.

Sinking Trick

Loons do not always dive to escape danger. A swimming loon can also sink in the water so that most of its body is below the surface. To do that it squeezes its feathers more tightly against its body to push out the air trapped between them. At the same time, it breathes out, so it has very little air in its **lungs**. With less air to keep it afloat, the loon sinks under its own weight until only its head and back can be seen. This trick helps it hide more easily among reeds and other water plants. When the danger is past, the loon takes a deep breath and bobs up again, like a floating cork.

Fish Hunter

Some waterbirds, such as herons, watch and wait for fish to swim close by. Then they catch and eat them. Herons may wait a long time for a meal. But a loon is not so patient. Instead of waiting for fish to come its way, the loon dives into the water and chases after them.

The loon swims so fast that it can easily overtake the small fish that it usually eats. The fish twist and turn as they try to escape. But the loon can twist and turn, too. The bird catches the fish with its sharp beak and often swallows them underwater with a single gulp. Loons bring bigger fish to the surface, but still swallow them whole. They also eat other animals, including frogs and crayfish—but fish are a loon's favorite prey.

Taking Off

Most birds have hollow bones. Hollow bones are very light, which makes flying easier. The bones of loons are solid, however. That makes them less likely to bob to the surface when they are hunting underwater. Therefore loons are heavier than most other birds of the same size. Compared with the size of its body, a loon's wings are on the small size. So, although a loon can fly quite well, it has real trouble getting into the air.

A loon manages to take off by running across the water with its webbed feet. It flaps its wings as quickly as possible until it is traveling fast enough to rise. A loon needs a long runway, just as a heavy aircraft does. The bird also needs a lot of space to land. It must keep flying fast on the way down, otherwise it simply falls out of the air. On a normal landing, a loon swoops low over the lake and then flops into the water in a cloud of spray.

A common loon
flaps its wings wildly
as it tries to take off.

In the Air

Once a loon has managed to take off, it flies using fast wing beats. It has to flap its wings quickly just to stay in the air. That is because its slender, pointed wings are barely large enough to lift its weight. While airborne, the loon holds its head lower than its body. Its feet stick out straight behind its tiny tail. That gives the bird an unusual humpbacked shape—and makes it look quite different from a flying duck. The only other birds that fly like that are grebes. However, loons often fly much higher than grebes, especially when they are traveling long distances.

A red-throated
loon has a
streamlined
shape as it flies.

A common loon
calls out to its mate.

Laughing Loons

In summer, male and female loons form pairs. The pairs will **mate** and nest on the fringes of northern lakes. Each pair of loons claims its own breeding **territory**, which is often an entire lake. They do that to make sure that they have enough food for themselves and their young. There may be more than one pair of loons on a large lake, but each pair stays in its own territory.

The male and female keep in touch by making laughing "ha-ha-ha" calls. They also give a ghostly, wailing "hoo-hoo-hoo-hoo-o-o-o" that can often be heard echoing over lakes on summer evenings. These calls also tell other loons that they are there. The calls warn neighbors not to **trespass** on their territory.

Dance or Fight?

Each loon stays with the same mate for life. Once a pair of loons has raised a family, they return to the same lake each summer to meet and breed again. When the loons meet, they perform a quiet dance on the water. They swim together slowly, each turning its head from side to side. They often dive together, too.

If their territory is invaded by other loons, the breeding pair gets much more excited. Rival males will rear up in the water with their wings outspread and start to fight. They jab at each other with their sharp beaks. Both the male and female chase intruders across the water and often attack them. Sometimes one loon stabs another and injures it so badly that it dies.

Red-throated loons fight over territory during the breeding season.

Two Arctic loon eggs lie side by side in a nest.

34

Lakeside Nest

Loons often nest in the same place each year, perhaps on a small island or a place where the land juts out into the lake. The birds have to be able to reach the nest easily from the water. They choose a place with a good view, so they can keep watch for any approaching danger. The loons pile up reeds and other plants to make the nest, shaping them into a shallow dish.

When the nest is ready, the female lays two eggs. They are about twice as big as hens' eggs and greenish brown with dark spots. This coloration makes the eggs more difficult to see. The **camouflage** helps protect the eggs from hungry predators, such as skunks and raccoons. If they can't see them, they can't eat them!

Egg Carers

Male and female loons take turns looking after their eggs and keeping them warm. Each parent sits on the eggs for two to four hours, while the other one hunts on the lake. Then they swap jobs. They **incubate** the eggs like that for about a month, until the eggs **hatch**.

The parent birds have to keep a constant watch for danger while they are on the nest. Many animals would like to eat the eggs. Some large predators might even attack the adult loons. If the parents feel threatened, they usually dive off the nest and into the water. The loons may splash noisily to attract their enemies away from the eggs. Often animals do not realize that the eggs are there because they are so well hidden.

Feathers fluffed,
a common loon
incubates its eggs.

37

A common loon chick sits beside a hatching egg.

38

Downy Chicks

Mother loons lay one egg at a time. The first egg that is laid is usually the first to hatch. The chick chips away at the shell from the inside, using its **egg tooth**. Eventually the baby loon breaks the eggshell so that it can get out. At first, the chick is wet and sticky. But it soon dries into a ball of fluffy black **down** with a white belly. The chick can see well and is curiously looking around the nest in no time.

If a predator finds an eggshell, it will know that chicks and a nest are nearby. So to deter predators, one of the parents takes the empty eggshell and drops it in the lake, where it is washed away.

Diving School

A few hours after hatching, the baby loons follow their mother and father out onto the lake. The chicks immediately know how to swim. But they find diving much more difficult. Because their downy feathers hold so much air, as the chicks try to dive down, the trapped air in their feathers pulls them back to the surface. Gradually, they get better at diving. By the end of their first week, the chicks can dive to the bottom and chase fish. But catching the fish is another story all together. Until the chicks can successfully hunt for themselves, the parents continue to feed them.

At about eight weeks old, the chicks have their first proper feathers. They are grayish and look like the dull winter coat of adult loons. By the time they are three months old, the chicks can fly. They are now ready to leave the lake and spend winter somewhere warmer.

A Pacific loon chick swims beside its parent on a lake.

A Pacific loon swims on an icy lake.

Escaping the Ice

As their lake starts to freeze over in late fall, the loons move south. They have to find open water where they can still hunt for fish. The adults usually leave first, and the young birds follow later. The birds stop at the first unfrozen lake they find. They stay there until that lake also starts to freeze and then leave to find another. Eventually, the loons find a lake that has open water all winter. Many loons also settle on seashores because the oceans (outside of the North and South Pole areas) never freeze.

They stay here until spring, often feeding in groups. Clean lakes with plenty of food can attract hundreds or even thousands of loons. These birds are not interested in defending a territory when they are not breeding.

New Feathers

In late winter, common loons molt their winter feathers and grow their summer plumage. But during this winter molt, the birds also lose the big flight feathers on their wings. It only takes a few days for the old feathers to drop out and the new ones to grow in again. But during this time loons cannot fly at all. The birds have to stay well away from the shore and their predators until their new flight feathers have grown and they can fly once more.

This red-throated loon will not be able to fly when its flight feathers molt.

A yellow-billed loon returns to its breeding lake in early spring.

46

Returning North

Loons seem to know when the ice is melting in the north because they arrive back in spring as soon as the ice has broken up. They set off early, traveling in stages, just as they did in fall. Moving from one lake to another, the birds make their way back to their summer home.

The young loons have to find homes of their own. They do not breed until they are at least four years old. Until that time, they just need to find a place to live where there is plenty of food. When they are old enough, the young loons find a mate, set up their own territory, and raise their first family. But this territory may be a long way from the lake where they were born.

Loon Love

Everybody seems to love loons. In the 1970s, people realized that loons were becoming rare in some places. So, they formed special groups to help protect them. One group is known as the Loon Rangers! People join these groups to tell others about loons, help study the birds, and look after their habitats—the places where the birds live. They even raise money to build floating nest platforms in places where there are not many good natural nesting sites.

The efforts of loon lovers have helped! Loons are surviving longer and raising more young. As a result, loons are becoming more common. You can now regularly see and hear loons on lakes where they were once just rare visitors.

Words to Know

Breed   To produce young.

Camouflage   Special patterns and colors that make an animal difficult to see against a particular background.

Down   Very soft, fluffy feathers.

Egg tooth   Toothlike point on the end of a chick's beak used to break out of the egg.

Hatch   To break out of an egg.

Incubate   To keep an egg warm, so the chick grows properly inside.

Lungs   Organs with which a bird breathes.

Migrate   Travel regularly from one home to another, usually in spring and fall.

Mate   To come together to produce young.

Molts Loses feathers before new ones grow back.

Plumage The feathers of a bird.

Preen gland An organ that produces oil, which a bird uses to clean and waterproof its feathers.

Predators Animals that hunt other animals.

Streamlined Describes a smooth, sleek shape that moves through water or air easily.

Territory An area that birds defend against neighbors, to keep their nest safe and make sure that they have enough to eat.

Trespass To go into an area that is occupied by others.

Webbed feet Feet that have skin stretched between the toes.

Find Out More

Books

Diehl, J. H. and K. Freeman. *Loon Chase*. Mount Pleasant, South Carolina: Sylvan Dell Publishing, 2006.

Lang, A. and W. Lynch. *Loons*. Thunder Bay, California: Thunder Bay Press, 2000.

Web sites

All About Birds

www.birds.cornell.edu/AllAboutBirds/BirdGuide/Common_Loon.html

Listen to the call of the common loon.

Everything About Loons

birding.about.com/od/birdsloons/Birds_Everything_About_Loons.htm

Facts and photographs about loons and their behavior.

Index